For

the Luck
of the
Irish

Compiled by
Patrick Kennedy, Marc Anello,
and Jordan Hayes

PETER PAUPER PRESS, INC.
WHITE PLAINS, NEW YORK

Copyright © 1996
Peter Pauper Press, Inc.
202 Mamaroneck Avenue
White Plains, NY 10601
All rights reserved
ISBN 0-88088-794-X

Book design by Susan Hood

Printed in Hong Kong
7 6 5 4 3 2

The Luck of the Irish

It's beautiful today. The luck of the Irish is with us.

Danny McAuliffe,
looking up at the sky
on St. Patrick's Day

Irish faces are artworks, monu-
ments to Irishness . . .

And the names! What is it about
Irish names, particularly boys'
names, regardless of last names? . . .

You get the feeling it's the mothers who give them to the sons, at least—that they like the thought of having a Brian or Kevin for a son—loyal, brooding, unpredictable, angry, funny, cute, solemn and chaste, even if he takes a drink now and then.

Henry Allen

She said he was an Irish lad.
Oh, really!
No — O'Reilly.

Mildred Meiers and
Jack Knapp

Once upon a time, thousands of years ago, when the country was inhabited by a race of wizards and sorcerers, the three kings who ruled there were married to three sisters. Each of the sisters was beautiful and each in turn gave her name to the country. One of these sisters was called Banba, another Fodhla and the third, Eire. And it was from Eire Ireland got her name.

James Plunkett

It's always a tradition for us. We're Irish on my mother's side. All of the girls have the middle name Burns. It's my mother's last name. And she makes sure they're aware of their Irish heritage.

Ann Kibble, speaking of her daughters Mary, Molly, and Maggy

How gallantly, indeed, do Irish wit, and cheerfulness, and hospitality, and patriotism ride on the wreck of individual hopes, and sparkle through the very waves of adversity!

Samuel G. Goodrich

The Irish have the best hearts in the three kingdoms.

Horace Walpole

There came to the beach a poor
   Exile of Erin . . .
Green be thy fields, sweetest isle
   of the ocean!
And thy harp-striking bards sing
   aloud with devotion,—
"Erin mavourneen—Erin go bragh!"

Thomas Campbell
EXILE OF ERIN

Translating Irish humor onto the printed page . . . is like trying to take home a handful of mist. So much of charm is in the ambience.

David Dempsey

Overheard in the Dublin bus terminal: Traveller: "I want a return ticket." Ticket seller: "Where to?" Traveller: "Back here, of course."

John McCarthy

My father told me, "If you miss an Irish parade, you aren't Irish."

William Heise

Notice in a Galway pub: Credit might be considered for *only* those over 85 accompanied by both their parents and a grand-parent.

John McCarthy

Some years ago, an Irishman from New Ross traveled to Washington. In order to let his neighbors know how well he was doing, he had his picture taken in front of the White House. On the back of the picture, he wrote, "This is my summer home. Come and see it."

John Fitzgerald Kennedy

Someone asked him if the caddy business slacked off a bit when the summer tourist season came to a close. "Well, we get some Japanese in the off season," he said, pondering the question through knitted brows. "But you know at times it's that quiet you can hear the bees belch."

Hugh A. Mulligan

I have had seatmates on a Dublin bus miss their stop because they had involved themselves too deeply in talk; it was more important to finish the joke—no such thing as a brief one, either—than to get off the bus.

David Dempsey

I will go with my father a-
ploughing
To the green field by the sea,
And the rooks and the crows
    and the seagulls
Will come flocking after me.
I will sing to the patient horses
With the lark in the white of the
    air,
And my father will sing the
    plough-song
That blesses the cleaving share.

John Campbell,
I Will Go with My Father
A-Ploughing

The harp, the shamrock, the ancient kings and the Round Towers of Other Days became symbols of Irish identity. Hitherto they had been part of the furniture, so to speak; now they were sacred remnants of a golden age, God's covenant with the Irish race.

James Plunkett

Maybe it's bred in the bone, but the sound of pipes is a little bit of heaven to some of us.

Nancy Q. Keefe

When the Irish moved West, they packed light. . . . They brought their stories, their dreams—and their musical instruments. "That was one of the only transportable parts of our culture," says Hal Ketchum.

Mike Hughes

On she went, and her maiden
smile
In safety lighted her round the
Green Isle;
And blest forever was she who
relied
Upon Erin's honour and Erin's
pride.

Thomas Moore

George Bernard Shaw, speaking as an Irishman, summed up an approach to life: "Other people," he said, "see things and . . . say: 'Why?' . . . But I dream things that never were—and I say 'Why not?'" It is that quality of the Irish—that remarkable combination of hope, confidence, and imagination . . .

John Fitzgerald Kennedy

There is no language like the Irish for soothing and quieting.

John Millington Synge

I am of Ireland,
And of the holy land
  Of Ireland.
Good Sir, pray I thee,
For of *saint charité*
Come and dance with me
  In Ireland.

THE IRISH DANCER,
14th century

Go slowly through the herds of cattle, stop and let the sheep flow by.

Eugene McCarthy, on driving in Ireland

O Ireland, isn't it grand you
   look—
Like a bride in her rich
   adornin'?
And with all the pent-up love of
   my heart
I bid you the top o' the mornin'!

John Locke,
THE EXILE'S RETURN

Up the airy mountain,
   Down the rushy glen,
We daren't go a-hunting
   For fear of little men;
Wee folk, good folk,
   Trooping all together;
Green jacket, red cap,
   And white owl's feather!

William Allingham,
THE FAIRIES

Dullness is the coming of age of seriousness.

Oscar Wilde

I could then go to a fair, or a wake, or dance. . . . I could spend the winter nights in a neighbor's house, cracking jokes by the turf fire. If I had there but a sore head I could have a neighbor within every hundred yards that would run to see me.

Letter from an Irishman in Missouri, referring to his homeland (1860)

There's a dear little plant that
   grows in our isle,
'Twas St. Patrick himself sure
   that set it: . . .
The sweet little shamrock, the
   dear little shamrock,
The sweet little, green little,
   shamrock of Ireland!

Andrew Cherry,
THE GREEN LITTLE SHAMROCK
OF IRELAND

To many of the Irish, whether in Ireland or in New York City, a pub is not just a bar, a place to grab a bottle of beer or a pint of Guinness stout, dark and bitter, yeasty and filling. In Ireland, a pub is the cultural epicenter, *the* place where people go at night.

Elaine Louie

Being Irish 365 days of the year means you don't compress all that Irishness into one day, as we do here in the States.

Washington Post

I admit this only one day a year, but the name Franey is actually Irish. In the 18th century there was a large Irish emigration to France, and many families settled in Burgundy. The name Franey has been traced to that time, although over the centuries those Irish immigrants became as French as a beret.

Pierre Franey

George Washington considered himself honored in being a member of an Irish society; that nine signers of the Declaration of Independence were men of Irish blood.

*American Irish
Historical Society*

Ladies and gentlemen, I don't want to give the impression that every member of my administration in Washington is Irish. It just seems that way.

John Fitzgerald Kennedy

I'm actually part Irish and I've often been accused of having a certain gift for blarney, though those were not the words used.

Bill Clinton

All politicians are 100 percent Irish on St. Patrick's Day. Humor, joy, good will and passion are Irish, and our cultures are intertwined.

Al Gore

I'm Irish today, but you never know what's going to happen on Columbus Day.

Peter F. Vallone

Each year on March 17 green cabbage enjoys its finest hour.

Jack Murdich

St. Patrick's Day is an enchanted time—a day to begin transforming winter's dreams into summer's magic.

Adrienne Cook

I marched in my first St. Patrick's Day parade in 1922 and I haven't missed one since. I'm 77 years old but I can still find the bars in the Channel.

Red Jack Burns

On St. Patrick's Day you should spend time with saints and scholars.

Ronald Reagan

The three best things: a little seed in good soil, a few cows in good grass, a few friends in the tavern.

Irish proverb

Wine comes in at the mouth
And love comes in at the eye;
That's all we shall know for truth
Before we grow old and die.
I lift the glass to my mouth,
I look at you, and I sigh.

William Butler Yeats,
A DRINKING SONG

Health and life to you;
The mate of your choice to you;
Land without rent to you,
And death in Eirinn.

Traditional toast

Experience is the name everyone gives to their mistakes.

Oscar Wilde

May you have warm words on a cold evening, a full moon on a dark night, and a smooth road all the way to your door.

Irish toast

May you be poor in misfortune,
rich in blessings,
slow to make enemies,
quick to make friends.
But rich or poor, quick or slow,
may you know nothing but happiness
from this day forward.

Irish toast

Golden butter on a new-made dish, such as Mary set before Christ. This is to be given in the presence of a mill, of a stream, and the presence of a tree, the lover saying softly: "O woman, loved by me, mayst thou give me thy heart, thy soul and body. Amen."

Traditional charm for love

Oh! an Irishman's heart is as
   stout as shillelagh,
It beats with delight to chase
   sorrow and woe;
When the piper plays up, then it
   dances as gaily,
And thumps with a whack to
   leather a foe.

Old Irish song

You know what they call the obituaries, don't you? The Irish sports page.

Danny Coleman

Back home in Syracuse, my brother Michael goes to four and five wakes a week. Wouldn't miss one. I say, "Michael, who's this one for?" He says, "That guy's father was our mailman when we were little. I think the family should be represented."

Danny Coleman

He was only forty-four years old and a real Irishman. I buried him in a green coffin, in a dark green suit and a green carnation.

Christine Cox,
Miss Liberty '86, speaking of her father

I come from a long line of Irishmen and Irishwomen and one thing my people have always done well is to send their dead off with colors flying, tin whistles playing and great street murmurs that almost always sound like this, "Ahh, he (she) never looked better."

Dennis Duggan

Ireland is rich in literature that understands a soul's yearnings, and dancing that understands a happy heart.

Margaret Jackson

Oh, list to the lay of a poor
  Irish harper,
And scorn not the strains of his
  old withered hand,
But remember those fingers they
  could once move sharper
To raise the merry strains of his
  dear native land . . .

Bold Phelim Brady,
THE BARD OF ARMAGH

We weave the shamrock into a garland of glory for the Emerald Isle, the home of scholars, the abode of poetry, the nursery of patriots and the Isle of the Saint.

Thomas Foley

With honey and with milk flow
  Ireland's lovely plains
With silk and arms, abundant
  fruit, strong women and men
Worthy are the Irish to dwell in
  this their land,
A race of men renowned in war;
  in peace, in faith.

St. Donatus

Celtic women, for a couple of millennia, have been a hardy bunch. The truth is, I suspect, that many of their menfolk like them that way. I sure do.

Andrew M. Greeley

I have never felt at home really in the places I've been. I was brought up Irish, my grandmother was full of Irish expressions, and it was very striking when I got off the plane, the words came to me, "I'm home."

Marlon Brando

May the Irish mother ever remain enthroned in the hearts of children and she ever enjoy the smile of God.

Thomas Foley

Ireland's greatest export has always been her people.

Nancy Q. Keefe

Oh, Ireland is so green and lovely, land of saints and scholars.

Anonymous

Let us draw inspiration from all those men and women of Ireland who gave young minds and hearts that most precious of legacies: a love of language, a dream of freedom, a sense of hope. God bless us all.

The Rev. Joseph A. O'Hare

It is said the Irish get more Irish
the farther they get from Ireland.

Rowena Daly

There are two classes of people, those who are Irish and those who lack ambition.

Anthony O'Reilly